Trees Sticker Book

Jane Chisholm

Illustrated by Aziz Khan,
Annabel Milne & Peter Stebbing

Edited by Simon Tudhope
Designed by Leonard Le Rolland
Consultant: Dr Mark A. Spencer

How to use this book

Using the pictures and descriptions, try to match each sticker to the right tree. If you need help, there is an index and checklist at the back of the book. There's a list of difficult tree words on the same page, too. There are also spaces in each entry to note when and where you spot each tree.

Here are some of the words used to describe parts of a tree:

Broadleaved tree

Crown
Leaf
Vein
Lobe
Fruit

Conifer

Twig
Needles
Cone
Scale
Bract
Bark

Pines

Pine trees are evergreen conifers. This means they don't lose all their leaves at once in winter, and their fruits are woody cones. They have thin, needle-like leaves.

Shore pine

Tall, fast-growing trees. Clusters of small cones. Pairs of yellow-green needles on twisted shoots. Scaly bark. Sticky, bullet-shaped buds. 23m (75ft)

WHEN ....

WHERE ....

Shore pine

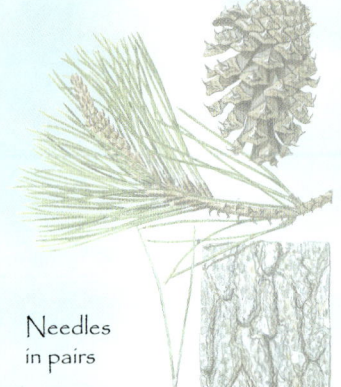

Needles in pairs

Long, bare trunk, red near the top

Scots pine

Pointed, green cones turn brown in second year

Scots pine

Short, blue-green paired needles. Small, pointed buds. Bark red at top; grey below. Young trees pointed in shape, flat-topped later. 35m (115ft)

WHEN ....

WHERE ....

Corsican pine

Tall, fast-growing trees. Branches at regular intervals. Long, dark green, paired needles. Onion-shaped buds. Large, lop-sided brown cones. Blackish bark. 36m (118ft)

WHEN ....

WHERE ....

Corsican pine

Cones take two years to ripen

Maritime pine

Native to Mediterranean. Often found in sandy soils near the sea. Long, stout, grey-green needles. Torpedo-shaped buds. Clusters of long, shiny brown cones. Long, bare trunk with rugged bark. 22m (72ft)

WHEN ....

WHERE ....

Long needles in pairs

Maritime pine

Cones stay on tree for several years

Monterey pine

From California. Broad crown with many branches. Slender, grass-green needles in threes. Large, pointed, sticky buds. Squat cones grow flat against branches and remain on tree for many years. 30m (98ft)

WHEN ....

WHERE ....

Monterey pine

Cones have uneven base

Swiss stone pine

Small for a pine. Found in the Alps and other mountainous areas. Wide, cone-shaped crown. Dense, stiff needles. Small, pointed, sticky buds. Egg-shaped cones. Seeds ripen and fall in their third year. 17m (56ft)

WHEN ....

WHERE ....

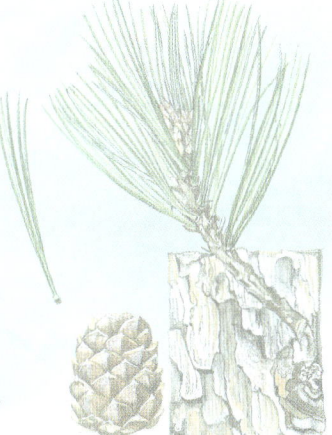

Swiss stone pine

Needles in fives

Spruces, firs and hemlocks

Spruces, firs and hemlocks are all evergreen conifers that bear cones and individual needles. Yews have berries, not cones.

Cones have papery scales with crinkled edges

Sitka spruce

Narrow, cone-shaped trees. Very prickly blue-green needles. Plump, yellow buds. When needles drop, they leave small knobs on yellow twigs. 35m (115ft)

WHEN ....

WHERE ....

Sitka spruce

Grey, scaly bark flakes off in "plates"

Norway spruce

Often used as Christmas trees. Regular, conical shape. Prickly, dark green needles, which leave peg-like bumps on brown twigs when they drop. Cones hang down. 30m (98ft)

WHEN ....

WHERE ....

Scales of cones tightly closed

Norway spruce

European silver fir

Common in central Europe. Tall and narrow. Flat needles (green above, silvery below) drop to leave flat, round scars on twigs. Ripe cones shed their scales. 40m (131ft)

WHEN ....

WHERE ....

Tall, upright cones

European silver fir

Tufts sticking out from cone are called bracts. They grow at the base of each scale.

Noble fir

Level branches. Dense, silver-blue needles curve upwards. Shaggy cones have down-turned bracts. Scales of cones fall off, leaving tall spikes. 37m (121ft)

WHEN ....

WHERE ....

Cones grow up to 20cm (8in) long

Douglas fir

Soft needles. Long, pointed copper-brown buds. Light brown hanging cones. Old trees have thick, corky bark. 40m (131ft)

WHEN ....

WHERE ....

Cones have three-pointed bracts

Yew

Often in churchyards or hedges. Short, stout trunk. Wide, spreading branches. Orange-brown, flaky bark. Red, berry-like fruits. Broad needles, dark green above, yellowish-green below. 15m (50ft)

WHEN ....

WHERE ....

Leaves and seeds are poisonous

Western hemlock

From western North America. Smooth, brown, scaly bark. Drooping branch tips and top shoots. Needles vary in length, and are green above, silver below. Small cones. 35m (115ft)

WHEN ....

WHERE ....

Older cones are brown

Young cones are green

Cedars and larches

Cedars and larches are conifers, but not all are evergreen. Most have single needles on new shoots, and bunches of needles on old shoots.

Cone with sunken top

Atlas cedar

Large, spreading tree from the Atlas mountains of Morocco. Often in parks and gardens. Branches rise upwards. Large, upright, barrel-shaped cones with sunken tops. 25m (82ft)

WHEN ....

WHERE ....

Atlas cedar

Blue-green leaves in common garden variety; dark green in wild

Cedar of Lebanon

Similar to Atlas cedars, but cones have rounded tops. Level branches with masses of dense foliage, giving the impression of flat "tables" of leaves. 30m (98ft)

WHEN ....

WHERE ....

Cedar of Lebanon

Cone covered with sticky resin

Deodar cedar

Pointed crown. Soft, pale green leaves. Top shoots and branches droop. Large, barrel-shaped cones with slightly sunken tops. 23m (76ft)

WHEN ....

WHERE ....

Deodar cedar

European larch

Deciduous. Bunches of soft, light green needles turn yellow and fall, leaving small knobs on twigs. Small yellow and larger reddish cones appear in early spring. Ripe cones are brown and egg-shaped and their scales lie flat. 38m (125ft)

WHEN ....

WHERE ....

European larches have fine, light branches

Japanese larch

Deciduous. Bunches of blue-green needles fall in winter, leaving orange twigs. Pinkish-green cones ripen to brown. Cone scales curl backwards like rose petals. 35m (115ft)

WHEN ....

WHERE ....

Japanese larches have stout branches

Ripe cone

Japanese red cedar

Tall and narrow. Cone-shaped, evergreen crown. Reddish-brown, peeling bark. Long, bright green, spiky scale-like needles curve away from the twig. Green, spiky cones turn brown when ripe. 30m (98ft)

WHEN ....

WHERE ....

Japanese red cedar

Reddish-brown peeling bark

7

Cypresses and redwoods

These conifers are all evergreen with sprays of scale-like leaves, apart from the dawn redwood and swamp cypress.

Western red cedar

A cypress from northwestern North America. Small, flower-shaped cones. Smooth, finely furrowed bark. Twigs covered with flat sprays of scented, scale-like leaves. 30m (98ft)

WHEN ....

WHERE ....

Western red cedar

Cone

Leaves dark, shiny green above, streaked white below

Monterey cypress

From California. Young trees are column-shaped; older ones are flat-topped. Dense sprays of small, scale-like leaves. Large, purplish-brown, rounded cones with knobs on scales. Bark often peeling. 25m (82ft)

WHEN ....

WHERE ....

Monterey cypress

Crushed leaves smell of lemon

Cone looks like a berry

Juniper

Juniper

Grows as trees or bushes. Prickly, blue-green needles smell strongly when crushed. Needles in threes, white band on upper surface. Berry-like cones turn purplish-black in second year. 20m (65ft)

WHEN ....

WHERE ....

Giant sequoia

World's largest tree. Also called sierra redwood or wellingtonia. Upswept branches. Soft, thick, deeply furrowed bark. Long-stalked, round, corky cones with diamond-shaped scales; wrinkle as they ripen. 30-90m (100-300ft)

WHEN ....

WHERE ....

Pointed, deep green, scale-like leaves

Giant sequoia

Dawn redwood

Cones grow on long stalks

Dawn redwood

Deciduous conifer. Soft, light green needles turn reddish in autumn. Cones rare, but when seen are small bobbles on long stalks. Bark orange when young; flaking and furrowed in older trees. 20m (66ft)

WHEN ....

WHERE ....

Swamp cypress

May grow in swamps. Crown triangular. Soft, feathery, light green needles drop in winter, leaving orange twigs. Round, purplish-brown cones. Reddish-brown bark, often peeling, forms a spiral pattern. 20m (66ft)

WHEN ....

WHERE ....

Swamp cypress

Thin foliage. Leaves appear very late

Simple leaves

Broadleaved trees have wide, flat leaves. The ones shown here have undivided ("simple") leaves.

Southern beech

Triangular crown. Slender, oval leaves, with finely toothed edges and many obvious veins. Deep green, prickly fruit. Silver-grey bark. 20m (66ft)

WHEN ....

WHERE ....

Southern beech

Common beech

In woods or parks. Spreading crown. Wavy-edged, oval leaves turn copper-brown in autumn. Smooth grey bark. Pointed nuts in hairy husks. 25m (82ft)

WHEN ....

WHERE ....

Common beech

Double-toothed edges

Silver birch

Slender, drooping branches. Silvery, peeling bark. Small "triangular" leaves. Long spikes of tiny flowers ("catkins") in winter. 15m (49ft)

WHEN ....

WHERE ....

Catkin

Silver birch

Common lime

Broad crown. Heart-shaped leaves with toothed edges. Yellow-green, scented flowers in July. Small, round, hard, grey-green fruits. 25m (82ft)

WHEN ....

WHERE ....

Fruits hang from a leafy wing

Silver lime

Woodland tree. Broad, rounded crown. Rounded leaves are dark green above, silvery-grey beneath. Small, round fruits hang from leafy wings. 20m (66ft)

WHEN ....

WHERE ....

Pointed leaf tip

English elm

Tall. Narrow, often uneven crown. Rough, oval leaves. Red flowers in clusters. Fruit winged, see-through, turning brown when ripe. 30m (98ft)

WHEN ....

WHERE ....

Leaves have double-toothed edges

Sweet chestnut

Large. Tall crown. Long, narrow leaves with saw-toothed edges. Clusters of edible brown chestnuts in prickly green cases. Bark may be spiral-furrowed. 25m (82ft)

WHEN ....

WHERE ....

Clusters of 2–3 fruits containing nuts

More trees with simple leaves

Grey alder

Fast-growing trees, with catkins and fruit rather like common alder (below). Pointed, oval leaves are soft and grey underneath, with sharply toothed and lobed edges. 14m (46ft)

WHEN ....

WHERE ....

Green, cone-like fruit is brown and woody when ripe

Grey alder

Common alder

Cone-like fruit stays on tree all winter

Common alder

Often grows near water. Rounded leaves fall in late autumn. Long yellow and short reddish catkins. Small, brown cone-like fruit. Young twigs and leaves are sticky. 12m (39ft)

WHEN ....

WHERE ....

Whitebeam

Often at edges of woods. Flowers and berries similar to rowan's, but ripen later. Large, oval leaves are white and furry underneath, with toothed edges. 8m (26ft)

WHEN ....

WHERE ....

Leaves white and furry underneath

Whitebeam

12

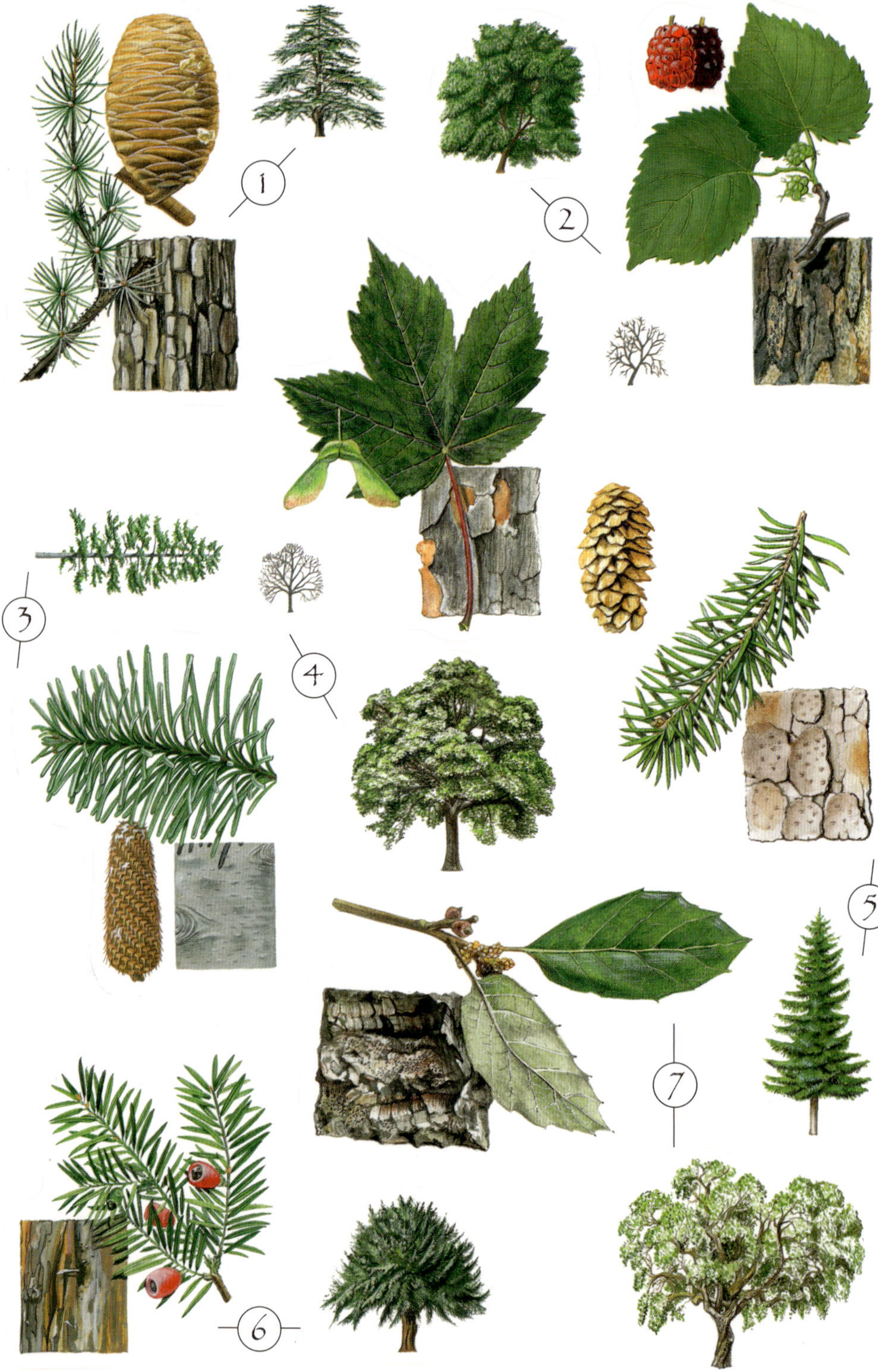
1
2
3
4
5
6
7

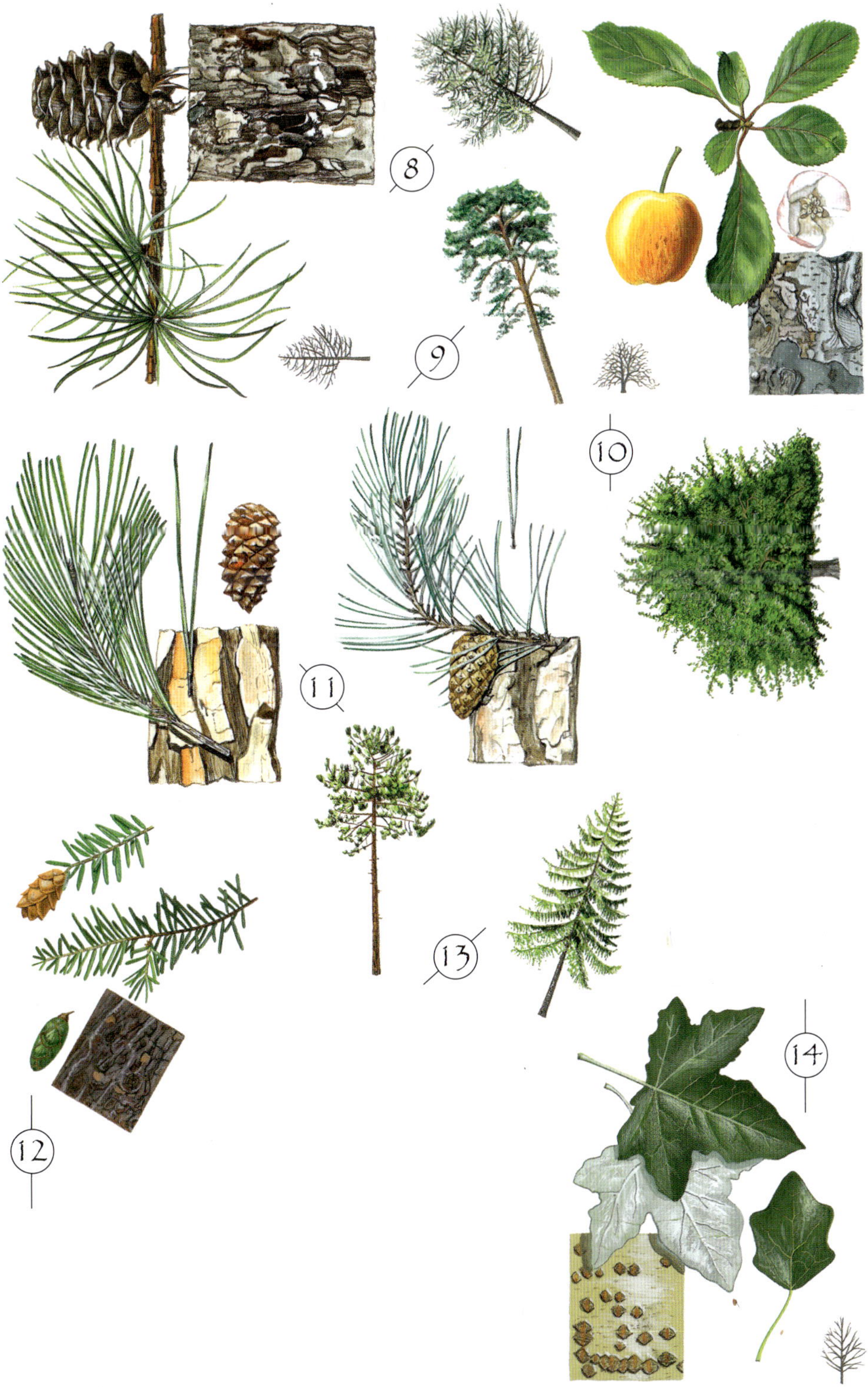

8
9
10
11
12
13
14

15
16
17
18
19
20
21

22

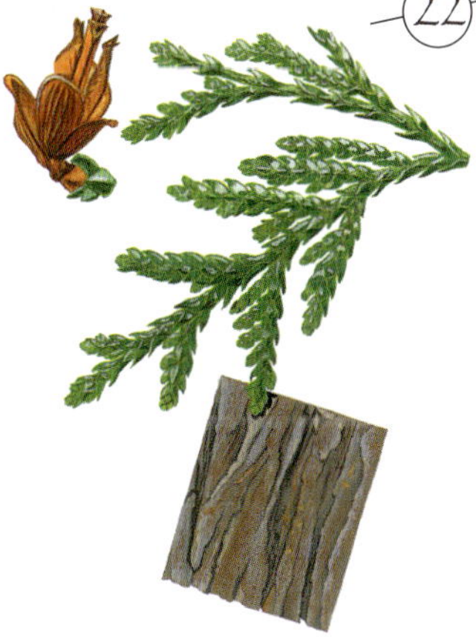

24

23

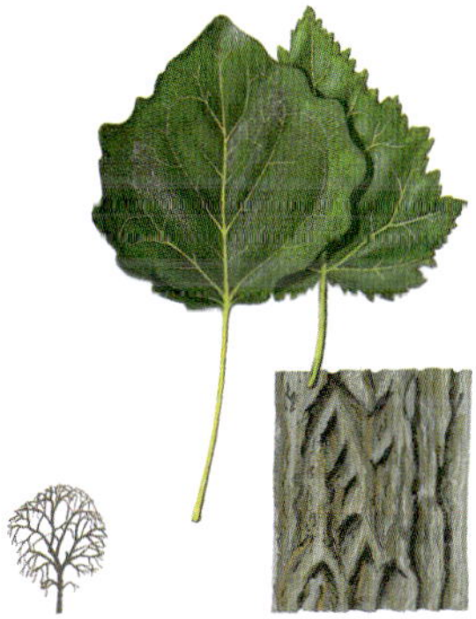

25

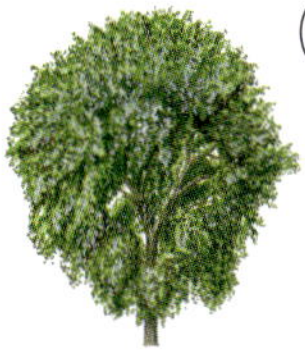

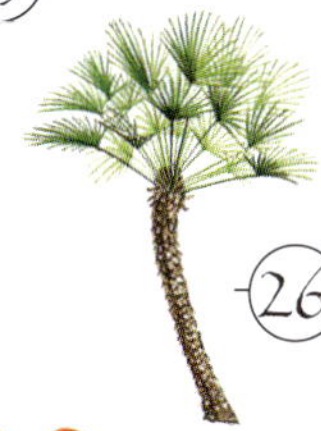

26

28

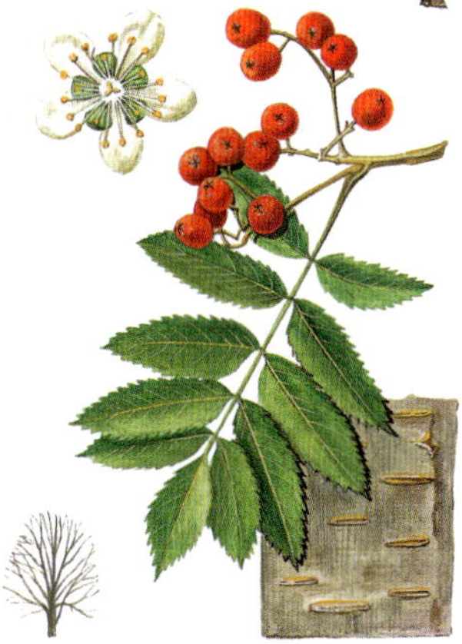

27

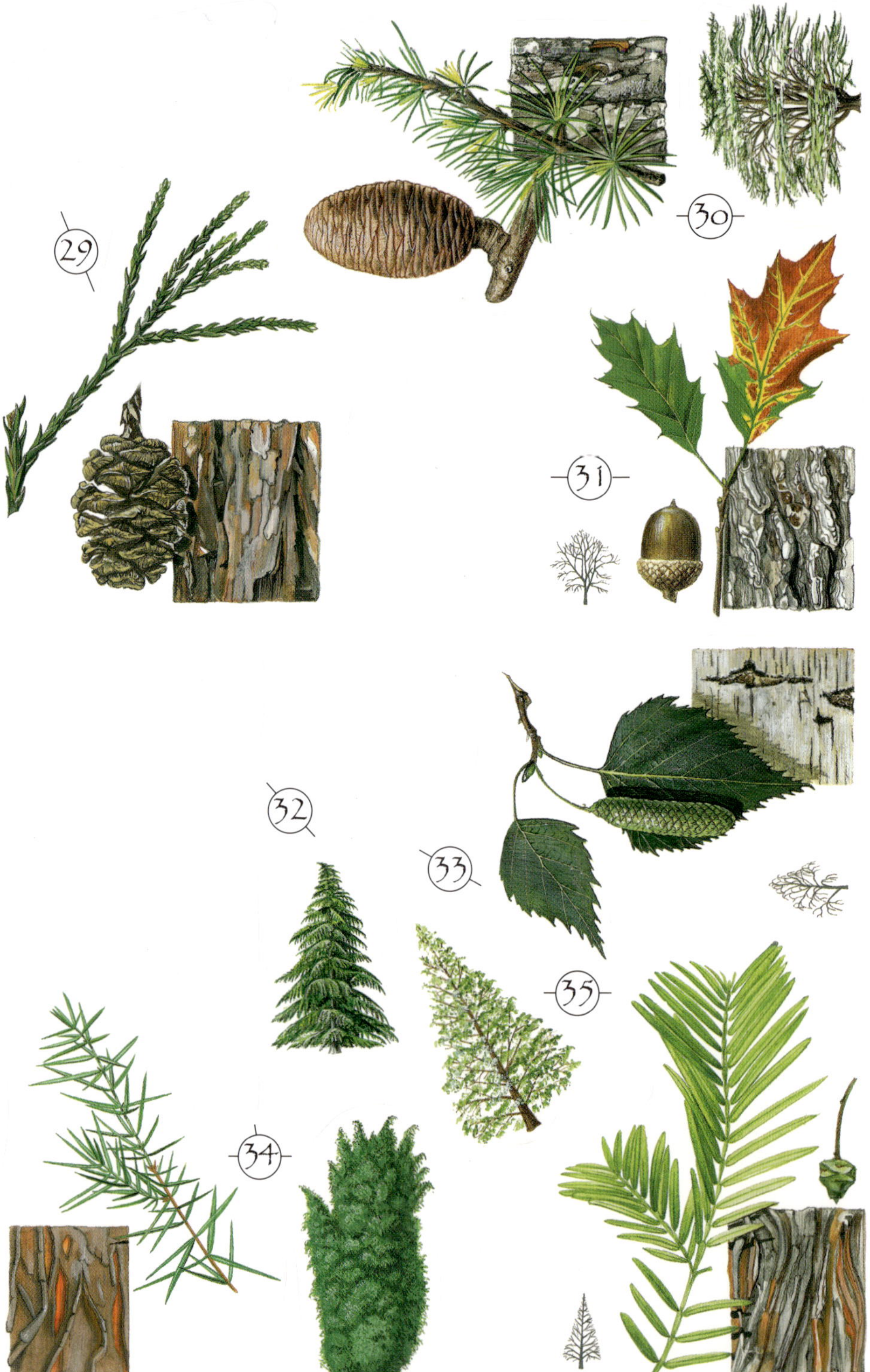
29
30
31
32
33
34
35

36 37
38 39
40 41 42

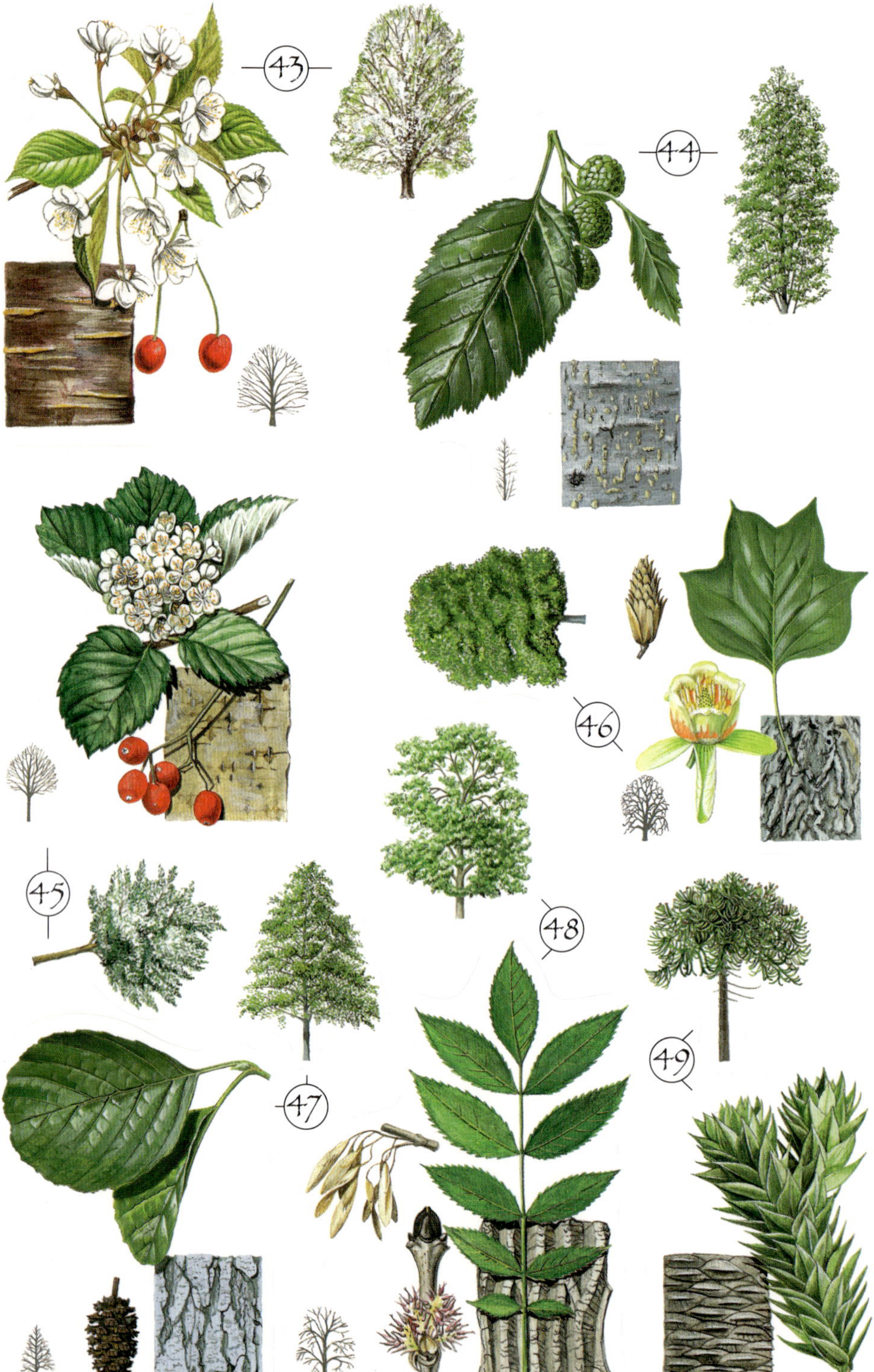

43
44
45
46
47
48
49

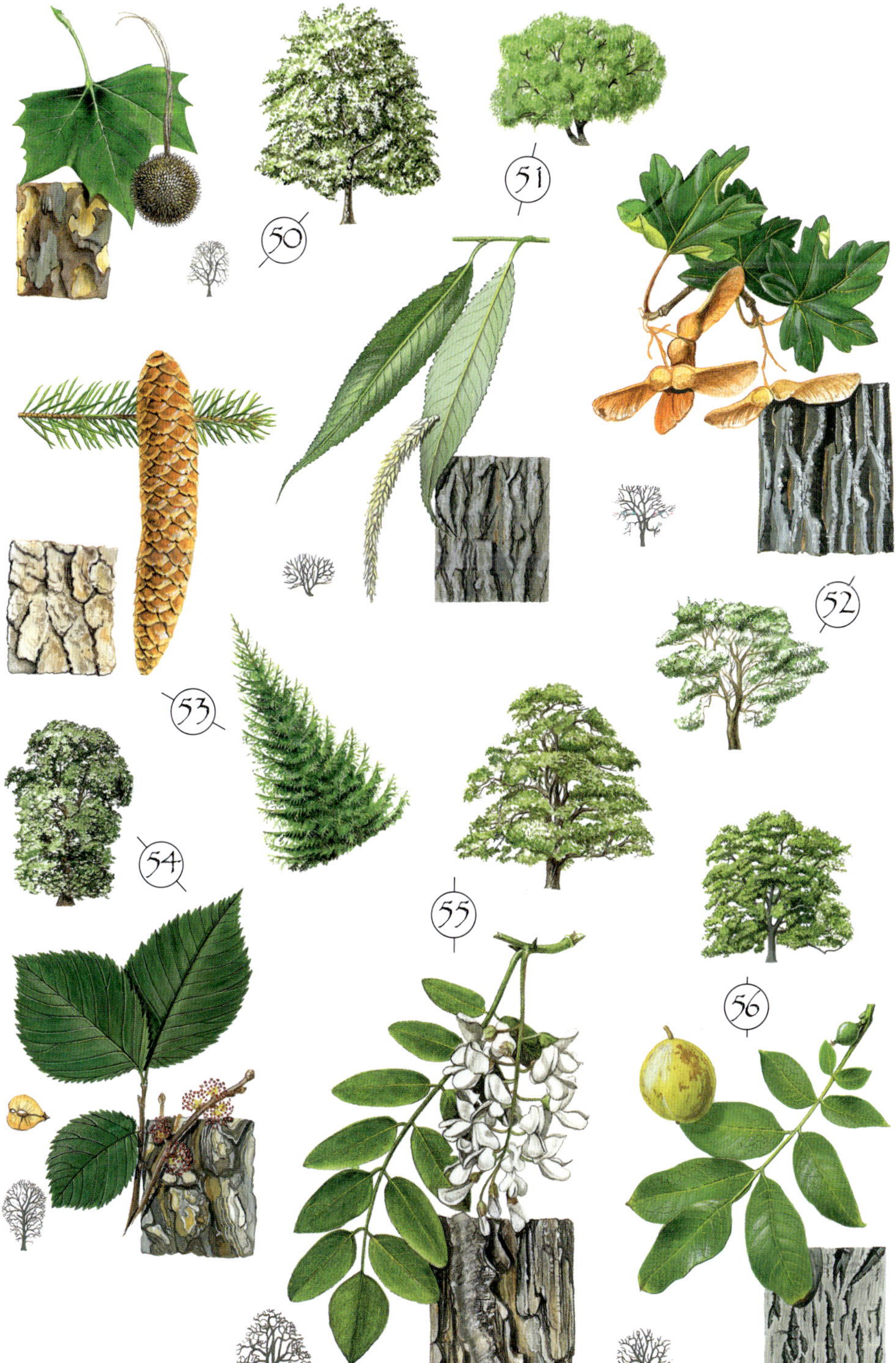
50
51
52
53
54
55
56

57
58
59
60
61
62

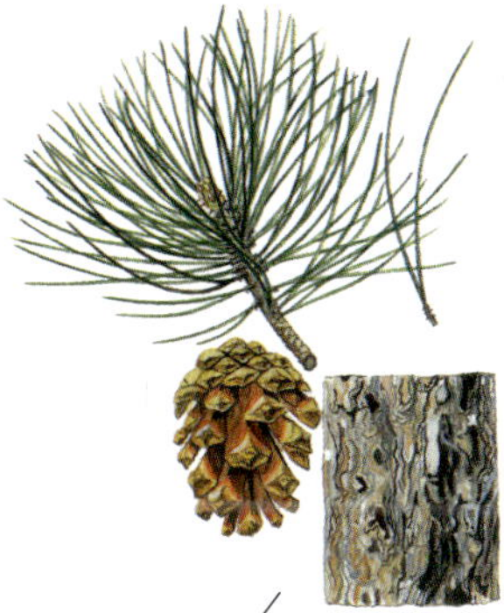

63

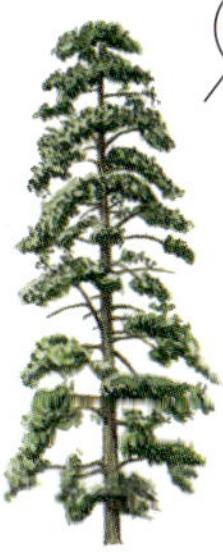

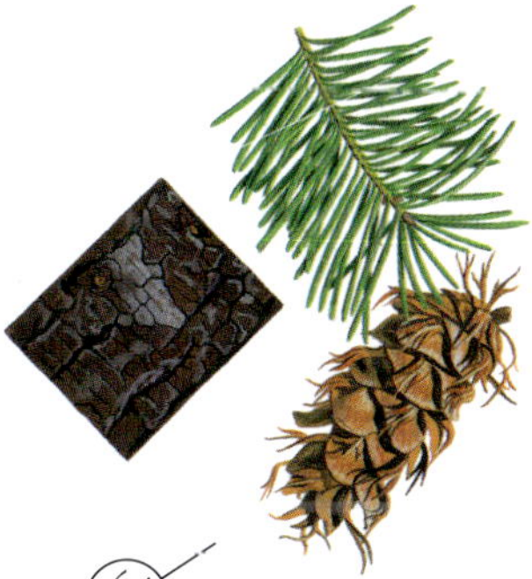

64

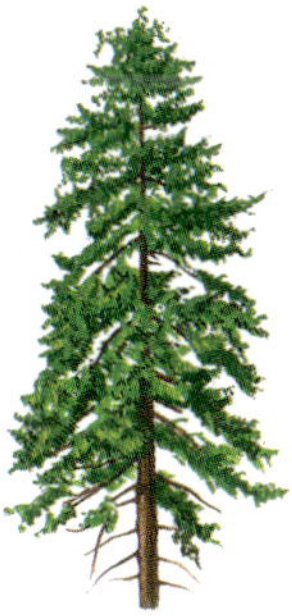

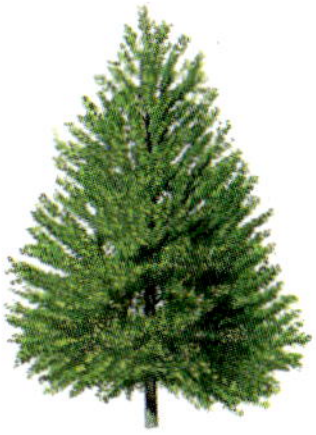

65

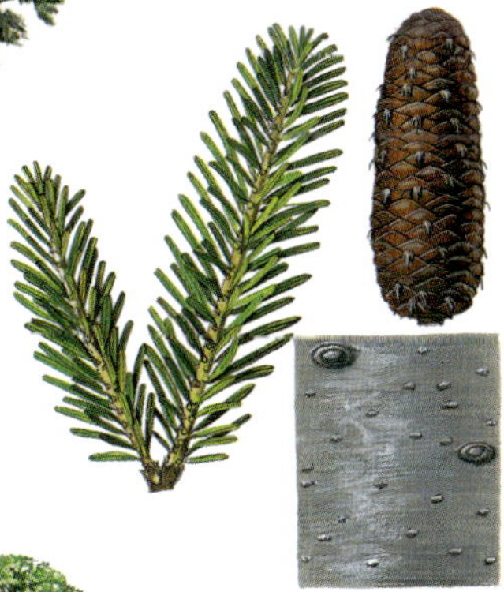

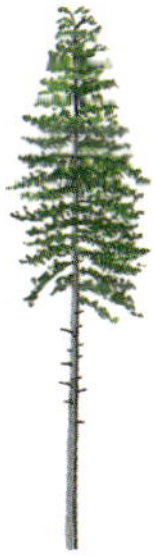

66

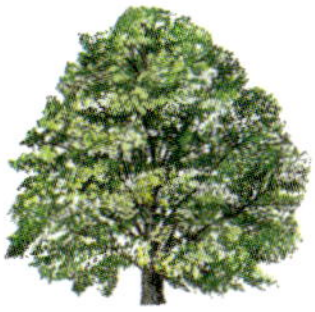

67

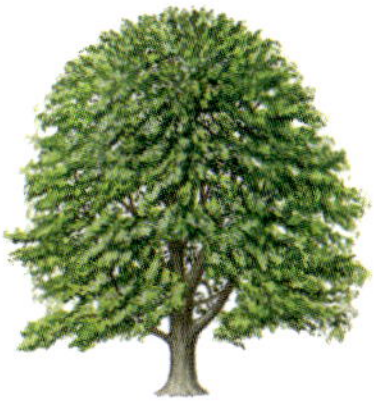

68

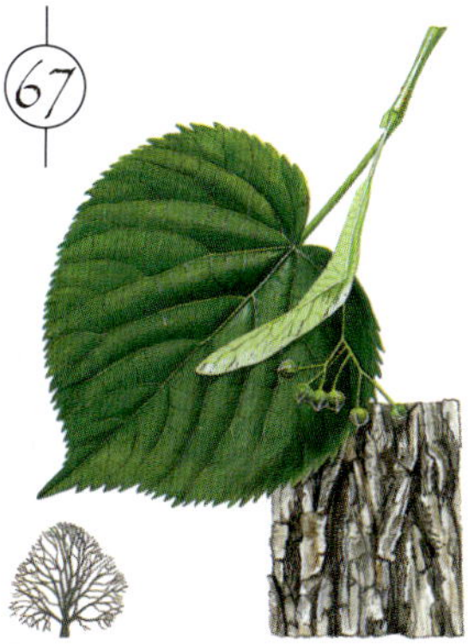

69

Common pear

Not very common. May be found in woods and hedgerows. Big, white flowers in April. Unripe pears gritty to eat, sweet when ripe. Small, dark green, oval leaves with finely toothed edges, long stalks. 15m (49ft)

WHEN ....

WHERE ....

Green pears turn golden when ripe

Leaves have toothed edges and pointed tips

Wild cherry

Blossom of white flowers in April. Large, dull green, oval leaves turn red in autumn. Reddish-brown bark peels in ribbons. Bitter-sweet cherries in mid-summer eaten by birds, but not usually by people. 15m (49ft)

WHEN ....

WHERE ....

Red cherries eaten by birds

Crab apple

Small, bushy trees found in hedgerows. Small, rounded leaves with toothed edges. Pinkish-white flowers in May. Small, reddish-green speckled apples too sour to eat raw, but used in cooking. 10m (33ft)

WHEN ....

WHERE ....

Sour-tasting apple

Oaks

Oaks are broadleaved trees with simple leaves. Many are deciduous, which means they lose their leaves in winter. They have fruits called acorns.

Sessile oak

Narrow crown. Thick, dark green, long-stalked leaves, tapering to the base. Acorns set close to twigs. 21m (69ft)

WHEN ....

WHERE ....

Sessile oak

Acorns more rounded than English oak

English oak

Tall acorns on long stalks

English oak

Broad crown. Broad, short trunk. Leaves on short stalks, with ear-like lobes at the base. 23m (75ft)

WHEN ....

WHERE ....

Holm oak

Common ornamental tree. Broad, dense crown. Unlike some oaks has shiny, evergreen leaves, greyish-green beneath. 20m (66ft)

WHEN ....

WHERE ....

Holm oak leaves vary in shape

Small acorns, almost covered by their cups

Red oak

Large leaves with bristly tipped lobes turn reddish-brown in autumn. Smooth, silvery bark. Squat acorns in shallow cups ripen in second year. 20m (66ft)

WHEN ....

WHERE ....

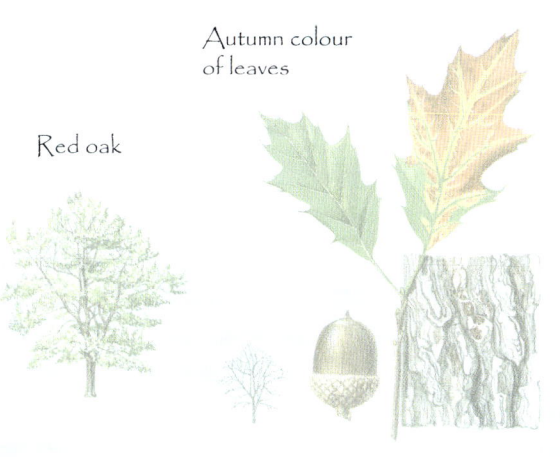

Autumn colour of leaves

Red oak

Turkey oak

Long, unevenly lobed leaves with whiskers at their base, and on buds. Stalkless, mossy acorn cups. Acorns ripen in second autumn. 25m (82ft)

WHEN ....

WHERE ....

Turkey oak

Mossy acorn cup

Cork oak

Smaller than other oaks. Evergreen, shiny leaves with wavy edges. Twisted trunk and branches. Thick, corky, whitish bark. Rare in Britain, common in southern Europe. 16m (52ft)

WHEN ....

WHERE ....

Cork oak

Tiny acorns

Bark used for cork

Poplars

Poplars are broadleaved, deciduous trees with simple leaves. Some bear hanging spikes of flowers called catkins.

Lombardy poplar

Tall and narrow. Furrowed bark. Branches grow upwards. Grows along roadsides in many parts of Europe. 28m (92ft)

WHEN ....

WHERE ....

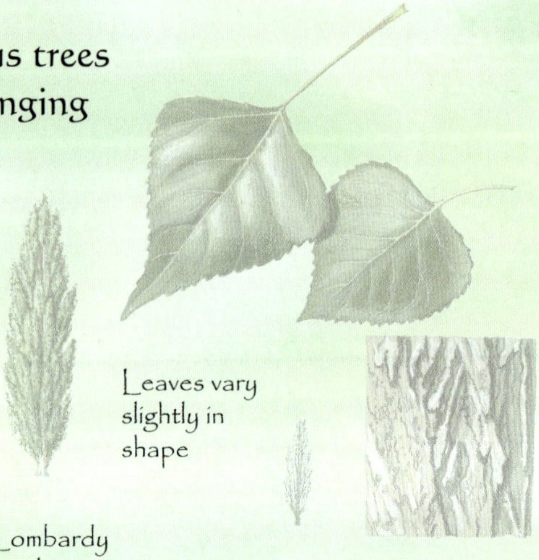

Leaves vary slightly in shape

Lombardy poplar

Black Italian poplar

Black poplar

Fast-growing. Trunk and fan-shaped crown often lean away from wind. Red catkins. Deeply furrowed bark. Dark green, tear-shaped leaves appear late in spring. Uncommon in Britain. 25m (82ft)

WHEN ....

WHERE ....

Leaf from lower branch

Leaf from upper branch

Grey poplar

Wavy-edged leaves are downy white underneath, but vary in shape up tree's length. Bark yellowish-grey at top; dark, furrowed below. 23m (75ft)

WHEN ....

WHERE ....

Grey poplar

Underside of leaf paler

Western balsam poplar

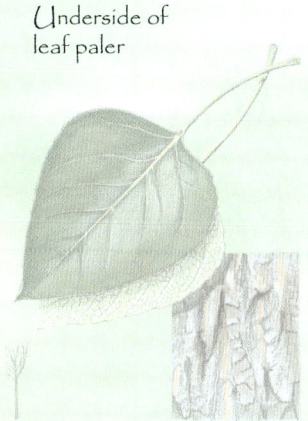

Western balsam poplar

Tall and fast-growing. Large, strawberry-shaped leaves paler underneath. White, fluffy seeds. Long, purplish catkins. 35m (115ft)

WHEN ....

WHERE ....

White poplar

White poplar

Similar to grey poplar. Often leans slightly. Leaves five-lobed and downy white lower down the tree; paler and more rugged nearer the top. Young trees have diamond shapes on bark. 20m (66ft)

WHEN ....

WHERE ....

Crown looks white because undersides of leave are pale

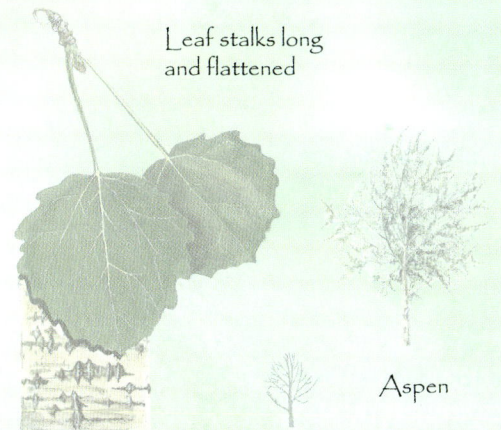

Leaf stalks long and flattened

Aspen

Aspen

Smaller than other poplars. Often found in woods. Grey bark with large pores. Rounded, wavy-edged, deep green leaves, paler underneath. Catkins purplish-grey and fluffy on some trees; white or green and woolly on others. 20m (66ft)

WHEN ....

WHERE ....

17

Willows

Willows are in the same family as poplars. They have catkins and simple, lobeless leaves.

Catkins known as pussy willow

Goat willow

Grows on damp waste ground. Small and bushy. Broad, rounded, rough grey-green leaves. Silvery-grey, upright catkins in late winter. 7m (23ft)

WHEN ....

WHERE ....

Goat willow

White willow

Catkins on female trees are white; male trees have yellow catkins

White willow

Grows by streams and rivers. Long, narrow, finely toothed leaves, white underneath. Slender, bendy twigs. 20m (66ft)

WHEN ....

WHERE ....

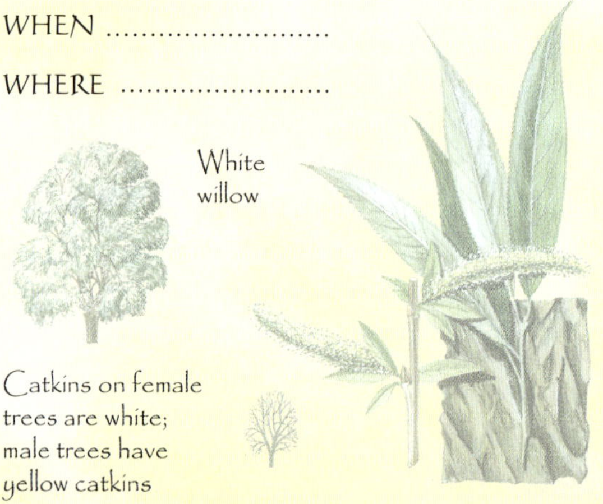

Crack willow

Very common willow. Grows near water. Often has branches cut back to trunk. Very long, narrow leaves, bright green above, grey-green below. Twigs easy to snap. 15m (49ft)

WHEN ....

WHERE ....

Very long, narrow leaves and catkins

Crack willow

Trees with lobed leaves

The trees on this page have lobed leaves, which are simple leaves that are partly divided into sections.

Leaves turn golden in autumn

Reddish winged fruit

Field maple

Small, round-headed tree. Often found in hedges. Small, dark green leaves with five lobes. Reddish, straight-winged fruit. 10m (33ft)

WHEN ....

WHERE ....

Field maple

London plane

Tall. Often found in towns. Broad, shiny, leaves. Spiny "bobble" fruits stay on tree all winter. Flaking bark leaves yellowish patches on trunk. 30m (98ft)

WHEN ....

WHERE ....

London plane

Leaves have toothed edges

Sycamore

Large. Smooth, brown bark, becoming scaly with age. Dark green, leathery leaves with five lobes. Bent-winged fruit spin as they fall. 20m (66ft)

WHEN ....

WHERE ....

Sycamore

19

Compound leaves

All these broadleaved trees have compound leaves, which are made up of smaller leaflets.

Seed clusters stay on tree into winter

Common ash

Woods, hedges and open hillsides. Leaves with 9 to 13 leaflets appear in late spring, after purplish flowers. Black buds. Pale grey bark. 25m (82ft)

WHEN ....

WHERE ....

Common ash

Fruit

Flowers grow in fluffy clusters

Manna ash

Smooth, dark grey bark. Leaves have between five and nine stalked leaflets. Clusters of white flowers in May. Seen in towns. 20m (66ft)

WHEN ....

WHERE ....

Manna ash

Rowan flower (from a cluster)

Rowan

Small. Often found alone on mountainsides, also in towns. Toothed leaves. Clusters of creamy-white flowers in May. Red berries in August. 7m (23ft)

WHEN ....

WHERE ....

Rowan

Common walnut

Broad-crowned tree. Edible walnuts grow inside smooth, green cases. Smooth, grey bark with some cracks. Leaves have seven to nine toothed leaflets. Hollow twigs. 15m (49ft)

WHEN ....

WHERE ....

Young leaves pinkish, turning green later

Common walnut

Pairs of thorns on twigs

False acacia

Leaflets have smooth edges

False acacia

Grows in sandy soil. Often has several trunks. Leaves have many small leaflets. Clusters of white flowers in June. Deeply furrowed bark. Seeds in pods. 20m (66ft)

WHEN ....

WHERE ....

Horse chestnut

Common in parks and avenues. Famous for brown, inedible "conkers" in green, spiny cases. Leaves have between five and seven large leaflets. Upright "candles" of white or pink flowers in May. 25m (82ft)

WHEN ....

WHERE ....

Horse chestnut

21

Unusual trees

The trees on these pages look distinctive. You'll only see some of them in parks and gardens.

Black mulberry

Low, broad crown. Short trunks. Rough, heart-shaped leaves. Twisted branches. Short, spiked flowers. Edible fruit. 15m (49ft)

WHEN ....

WHERE ....

Fruits ripen to red and purplish-black

Black mulberry

Grey bark flakes off in "plates"

European fan palm

Large, fan-shaped leaves, made of 12–15 stiff, pointed leaflets. Large clusters of small flowers and fruits. Rare in Britain. 4m (13ft)

WHEN ....

WHERE ....

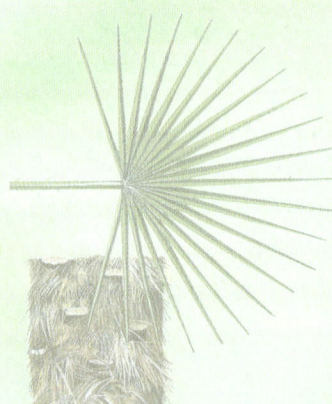

Only planted European fan palms have tall trunks

Holly

Small tree. Smooth, grey-green bark. Shiny, prickly, evergreen leaves. Small white flowers. Poisonous red berries in autumn and winter. 10m (33ft)

WHEN ....

WHERE ....

Berries only appear on female trees

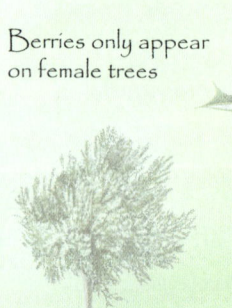

Holly

Tulip tree

Tall. Narrow crown. Smooth, four-lobed leaves turn golden in autumn. Flowers look like tulips. Upright, brown, cone-like fruits. 20m (66ft)

WHEN ....

WHERE ....

Leaves have squared lobes

Coast redwood

Californian. World's tallest tree. Thick, spongy, reddish bark. Hard needles dark green above and white-banded below. Small, round cones. 35-110m (115-360ft)

WHEN ....

WHERE ....

Needles parted either side of twig

Monkey puzzle

Broad, rounded crown. Pole-like trunk. Twisting branches. Stiff, leathery leaves with sharp points grow all around the shoots. Wrinkled bark. 23m (75ft)

WHEN ....

WHERE ....

Leaves overlap each other

Maidenhair

Neither conifer nor broadleaved, but in a group of its own. Double-lobed leaves turn bright yellow in autumn. Can have hanging fruits, like small plums. 23m (75ft)

WHEN ....

WHERE ....

Yellow, plum-like fruit

Index and checklist

This list will help you find every tree in the book. The first number after each tree tells you which page it is on. The second number (in brackets) is the number of the sticker.

Aspen 17 (19)
Atlas cedar 6 (1)
Black mulberry 22 (2)
Black poplar 16 (15)
Cedar of Lebanon 6 (30)
Chile pine (see Monkey puzzle)
Coast redwood 23 (18)
Common alder 12 (47)
Common ash 20 (48)
Common beech 10 (68)
Common lime 11 (67)
Common pear 13 (37)
Common walnut 21 (56)
Cork oak 15 (7)
Corsican pine 2 (63)
Crab apple 13 (10)
Crack willow 18 (51)
Dawn redwood 9 (35)
Deodar cedar 6 (32)
Douglas fir 5 (64)
English elm 11 (54)
English oak 14 (61)
European fan palm 22 (26)
European larch 7 (13)
European silver fir 4 (66)
False acacia 21 (55)
Field maple 19 (52)
Giant sequoia 9 (29)
Goat willow 18 (28)
Grey alder 12 (44)
Grey poplar 16 (25)
Holly 22 (41)
Holm oak 14 (39)
Horse chestnut 21 (16)
Japanese larch 7 (8)
Japanese red cedar 7 (38)
Juniper 8 (34)
Lombardy poplar 16 (20)
London plane 19 (50)
Maidenhair 23 (42)
Manna ash 20 (36)
Maritime pine 3 (11)
Monkey puzzle 23 (49)
Monterey cypress 8 (24)
Monterey pine 3 (62)
Noble fir 5 (3)
Norway spruce 4 (53)
Red oak 15 (31)
Rowan 20 (27)
Scots pine 2 (9)
Sessile oak 14 (57)
Shore pine 2 (59)
Sierra redwood (see Giant sequoia)
Silver birch 10 (33)
Silver lime 11 (69)
Sitka spruce 4 (5)
Southern beech 10 (65)
Swamp cypress 9 (40)
Sweet chestnut 11 (23)
Swiss stone pine 3 (17)
Sycamore 19 (4)
Tulip tree 23 (46)
Turkey oak 15 (58)
Wellingtonia (see Giant sequoia)
Western balsam poplar 17 (60)
Western hemlock 5 (12)
Western red cedar 8 (22)
Whitebeam 12 (45)
White poplar 17 (14)
White willow 18 (21)
Wild cherry 13 (43)
Yew 5 (6)

Tree words

Bract – on some cones, a leaf-like part that grows at the base of each scale

Broadleaved – a tree with wide, flat leaves. Most broadleaved trees are deciduous.

Bud – a swelling on a branch that grows into leaf-shoots or flowers

Compound leaf – a type of leaf that is divided into smaller "leaflets"

Conifer – a tree that bears cones containing its seeds. Most conifers are evergreen with needle-like leaves.

Crown – the leaves and branches at the top of a tree

Deciduous – a tree that sheds all its leaves every year at the end of the growing season

Evergreen – a tree that is covered with leaves all year round

Fruit – part of a tree that holds its seeds. It may take many forms, including berries, nuts, cones and winged seeds.

Hardwood – a name sometimes used for broadleaved trees

Leaflet – a section of a compound leaf

Lobed leaf – a type of simple leaf. Its partly divided sections have round edges.

Sapling – a young tree, over 1m (3¼ft) high, with a trunk up to 7cm (2¼in) around

Seedling – a newly sprouted tree, under 1m (3¼ft) high

Simple leaf – a type of leaf that is all in one piece

Softwood – a name sometimes used for conifers

Toothed leaf – a type of leaf with jagged edges

Additional design: Marc Maynard
Cover design: Karen Tomlins
Digital imaging: Keith Furnival

Cover images: © Graham Bell / Alamy, Tim Gartside / Alamy and 1997 Digital Vision Ltd.
This edition first published in 2010 by Usborne Publishing Ltd, Usborne House, 83–85 Saffron Hill, London EC1N 8RT, England. www.usborne.com © 2010, 2000 Usborne Publishing Ltd. The name Usborne and the devices ⓠ ⓟ are Trade Marks of Usborne Publishing Ltd. All rights reserved. No part of this publication may be reproduced, stored in a retrieval system, or transmitted in any form or by any means, electronic, mechanical, photocopying, recording or otherwise, without the prior permission of the publisher. Printed in Heshan, Guangdong, China.